Shoulders
-and-
Shadows

Shoulders
-and-
Shadows

Following Legendary Leaders

Selwyn Q. Bachus

Shoulders and Shadows by Selwyn Q. Bachus
Copyright © 2017 by Selwyn Q. Bachus
All Rights Reserved.
ISBN: 978-1-59755-453-4

Published by: ADVANTAGE BOOKS™
Longwood, Florida, USA
www.advbookstore.com

Interior Design by Jomar Ouano

Library of Congress Catalog Number: 2017942408
1. Religion / Leadership
2. Religion / Christian Life / Personal Growth

First Printing: June 2017
17 18 19 20 21 22 23   10 9 8 7 6 5 4 3 2 1
Printed in the United States of America

Acknowledgments

*T*o the Lord Jesus Christ, I say thank-you for the favor you have poured out in my life. I am eternally grateful.

I want to extend my heartfelt thanks to Marla C. Bachus, Selwyn Q. Bachus II, and Myles Christian Jerome Bachus—they have sacrificed to allow me to give loving leadership to congregations across the country.

I also want to thank Dr. C. L. and Dr. Wilma Bachus for being great examples of servant leaders. I extend my thanks to my siblings—Reginald, Verneda, Jerome, and Sonja for their support and encouragement.

To the First Union Baptist Church of Richmond, Virginia; the Shiloh Baptist Church of Dayton, Ohio; and the Salem Baptist Church of Omaha, Nebraska—I extend thanks from the depths of my heart for allowing me to serve you as pastor. It has been the pleasure of my life to provide leadership to each of you.

I am appreciative of the ministries, memories, and legacies of Dr. W. L. Henderson, Dr. Henry L. Parker, and Dr. Maurice Watson. It is upon their shoulders and in their shadows that I have taught, preached, and led. It has been a privilege to succeed each in ministry.

Contents

Introduction 9

1 The Ideal 21

    Training 22

    Transference of Authority 25

    Transference of Vision 27

2 The Realities the New Leader Faces 33

    Lack of Influence 36

        Influence Is Gained by Commitment
          to the Lord's People 36

        Influence Is Gained by Caring
          for the Lord's People 37

        Influence Is Gained by Consistency
          with the Lord's People 38

Influence Is Gained by Character
among the Lord's People 39

Lack of Experience.. 40

Lack of Exposure to a Successful Succession Model 46

3   The Reluctance of the Followers 49
Positional, Not Personal. 50
Loyalty to Prior Pastors... 56
Loyalty to Long-standing Relationships................. 60

4   Moving Forward in Faith.....................................65
Spiritually 67
Strategically 70
Confidently ....

Introduction

I was being prepared for operating in the shadows of great leaders before I was even aware of it. It was a function of whom I was born to. Both my parents were extraordinary leaders. My parents were born into the oppressive system of Jim Crow that dominated the southern states of the United States. They were born and raised in DeSoto County, Mississippi—Hernando, Mississippi, to be exact. My parents were exposed to the heavy hand of the cotton crops of the south. They both knew what picking cotton was all about. Yet, like thousands of African-Americans of their generation, these experiences did not strangle their ambition and drive; it fed and nurtured it. Determination and strength were evidenced in their drive for education and success. Neither of my parents had open opportunities for advanced education as youth and young adults. However, it did not suppress their longing for exposure and educational attainment. I remember, as a high school senior, celebrating with my mother as she was awarded her undergraduate degree the same weekend I received my high school diploma. The planets aligned once again as she was awarded her master's degree the same week I was awarded my bachelor's degree. She forged forward and is now Dr. Wilma Bachus after attaining her PhD.

As I said earlier, I was being prepared for operating in the shadow of great leaders before I was aware of it. My father's life and ministry cast a great shadow because of the giant of a man he is. Although not formally educated, he exposed himself to theological training even though he would not be technically awarded a degree. The training that allowed him to be recognized as a "doctor of the church" was the reward more than the actual paper degree. I have watched pastors and preachers both degreed and not figuratively sit at the feet of my father and receive wisdom and instruction from his experiences that no textbook could impart. My father's model of ministry is one that closely engages his congregation, the community, culture, and the larger denominational context. He has never been hands off. So imagine my formative years observing my father in his pastoral context. The congregation he gave leadership to reveres his leadership and covets his attention. He is a social and political influencer in the community in which he ministers. He is always sought out to speak truth to power even on very controversial issues, and he is never silent when it was important. He is dedicated to and fought for the beloved National Baptist Convention, USA, Inc. of which he is a leader. With all of that, he is a gifted preacher who can "say it!" As I struggled with my call to ministry, all of this caused me great pride and great trepidation. If I accepted my call to ministry, I would be very proud to be called my earthly father's "son in the ministry." However, how would I measure up as a young man who had not had many major struggles compared to a man who had made it from the cotton fields of Mississippi to become a nationally known preacher and pastor? How great the shoulders I would be standing upon and how great the shadow I would be standing in.

As I came to the boiling point of resisting the call of the Lord in my life, it finally overflowed, and I acknowledged what—it is apparent now—my father had observed many years prior. I shared with him the calling on my life and how his success in ministry had at times caused me to run from my call. He shared with me in the early hours of a Sunday morning that he had to preach, a few words of wisdom that have allowed me to navigate and operate in the shadows of him and my pastoral predecessors. I hope these words and this book will aid others in this very important task of leading the Lord's people whether in church or in other pursuits of life. My father said to me, "Son, the Lord decides who He calls, and no one else in the world, even me, can do anything about it." He then looked at me intently as tears welled up in his eyes and tears flowed down his face and said, "Selwyn, no one can be you better than you. Let the Lord develop you into the best you that you can be."

Those words of wisdom have guided me in my life and in my pastoral ministry. They have defined how I have sought to operate in the shadows of the three legendary leaders I have followed in pastoral ministry.

My first pastoral experience of operating in the shadow of a legendary leader was fresh out of seminary at the School of Theology of Virginia Union University in 1995. The previous summer, I had the opportunity to preach at the First Union Baptist Church, Dill Road, filling the pulpit in light of the pastor's death. As I drove off the parking lot, I told my wife that the Lord had called me to this church. She replied, "Don't say that because they may not call you."

My response was, "I don't have anything to do with that, but this is where the Lord wants me to be!" After going through the pastoral search process, I was called in June of 1995 to be the pastor of the First Union Baptist Church, Dill Road. First Union was a prized charge for a recent seminary graduate because it was a "city church" although it was located just a few hundred yards outside the Richmond City limits. Most recent seminarians' first pastoral opportunities were in rural churches, and so I was considerably blessed. At First Union, I followed Dr. W. L. Henderson who, at the time of his death, had served First Union for thirty-seven years. Dr. Henderson was a respected pastor among both congregants and clergy alike in Richmond. He was a great pulpiteer with a booming preaching voice and was known for his ability to stir the congregation with the great hymns of the church. Dr. Henderson was widely known as a popular revivalist throughout Virginia. Dr. Henderson was not just a preacher, he was a visionary leader. First Union had been located in the Newtown section of the city of Richmond just behind Maggie L. Walker High School. Dr. Henderson saw the writing on the wall. He knew the church could not expand at its current location, and he wanted to follow the population trend; therefore, he led the church to move to the fast-growing edge of the city into eastern Henrico County. It was this visionary move and his powerful preaching and leadership that endeared him to First Union. Succeeding this legend-ary leader was a pleasure although it was not without challenge. The largest of those challenges was my youth. I was twenty-seven years old, trying to lead a congrega-tion with people my parents' age and some old enough to be my parents' parents at the time. Standing in the shadow of a veteran pastor as a very young man was not an easy task. One of the great lessons I learned about operating in the shadow of a veteran predecessor is that the memory of the predecessor is near and dear to those you have inherited. To try to erase and eradicate his or her impact is a slap in the face of those you are trying to lead. I invited the congregation to have grand respect of my predecessor(s) while always having an eye toward the future. The Lord blessed First Union spiritually, numerically, and financially the five and a half years I was privileged to be their pastor.

My second experience of operating in the shadow of a legendary leader was as the pastor of the Historic Shiloh Baptist Church of Dayton, Ohio, that began in the spring of 2001. Once again, I followed a long-standing pastor of great influence. Dr. Henry L. Parker, Sr. served the Shiloh Church for twenty-seven years as pastor. Dr. Parker was an Alabama-born preacher with an abundance of gifts that make a preacher well respected. He was a gospel recording artist, a gifted preacher, and had an impact on the civil rights movement and through his community activism. He worked with Dr. Martin Luther King Jr., Rev. Jesse Jackson, and Rev. Fred Shuttlesworth to name a few. Dr. Parker had immeasurable influence in the work of the Baptist denomination in Ohio and was often the voice of the consciousness of that work. Dr. Parker transitioned into retirement after twenty-seven years of leading one of the most well-respected congregations in the country. I was blessed to inherit a proud congregation that had plateaued. Many of the necessary elements that could spur growth and rebirth in this congregation were present: a proud history, a strong music ministry, strong senior leaders, and a physical infrastructure that could accommodate explosive growth. He also had an element that might not be essential but was extremely helpful. Dr. Parker was always privately and publicly supportive and did not entertain naysayers. He also had such a prolific personal preaching ministry that he was so busy preaching it did not allow him time to muddle and meddle in the activities of the Shiloh Church. With those elements in place, Shiloh saw a turnaround that was a blessing to witness. In four short years, the budget more than doubled, average attendance tripled from three hundred to over nine hundred, and with the financial support and commitment of the congregation, we successfully carried out a floor-to-ceiling renovation of the sanctuary at a cost of $1,050,000. Even as I departed the Shiloh Church in the summer of 2005, I marveled at what the Lord had done and how he had allowed me to witness His power.

My third opportunity at operating in the shadow of a legendary leader has been my most rewarding and most challenging. It has strengthened my faith in and dependence on the Lord in a way none of my prior experiences could have. Leaving what was a national pulpit at the Shiloh Church had, to a degree, prepared me for what was at the Salem Baptist Church of Omaha, Nebraska, an international pulpit. I say that because internationally acclaimed preachers have graced the pulpit of the Salem Church for the last fifty years. Just five months after my arrival at Salem, Dr. Gardner C. Taylor, the prince of preachers, graced the pulpit of the Salem Church for the citywide Martin Luther King Jr. celebration. This might have been new to some, but to the congregation of the Salem Church, it was not out of the ordinary. Dr. J. C. Wade Sr. had pastored the Salem Church for approaching fifty years. And most recently and more impactful for me, I would preach each Sunday in the shadow of Dr. Maurice Watson in a multimillion dollar church edifice he had lead the congregation to build. Interesting how the Lord maneuvers and manages our lives and ministries. As a teenager struggling with my call to ministry, my father and the church he pastored visited the St. Mark Baptist Church of Little Rock, Arkansas. At the time, a young, gifted, and up-and-coming Maurice

Watson was the pastor. On that trip, I observed his congregation follow him as a young man. I watched older
men serve him and follow his directions. I encountered
him again just a few months later as Dr. Watson and
the St. Mark Church visited the Mt. Zion Church in
Kansas City, Kansas, where my father was pastor. It
was a sight to see a young man preach with such power
and intensity. And even years later, as I pastored the
Shiloh Church in Dayton, Ohio, Dr. Watson was the
revival preacher two years in a row. And now, I would
be preaching each Sunday in the edifice he built and in
the shadow of his ascending ministry. This was different.
In my prior two charges as pastor, I was thrust into a
plateaued or declining church context. The turnarounds
were exponential and measureable. The growth, at times,
was unmanageable. Now I was given the challenge to
lead a vibrant, acclaimed congregation wounded because
of the loss of their charismatic leader who the Lord had
led to a new challenge in ministry. Once again, I found
myself in the shadow of the ministry of a giant of a man.
I, once again, heard the words of my father from twenty
years prior as I started ministry. "Son, the Lord decides
who He calls. And no one else in the world, even me,

can do anything about it. Selwyn, no one can be you better than you. Let the Lord develop you into the best you that you can be." That is why when a reporter from the *Omaha World Herald* interviewed me and reminded me that Salem had been the largest African-American church in Nebraska for fifty years, and followed up that statement informing me of Dr. Wade's extensive tenure and Dr. Watson's nationwide preaching acclaim, and then followed up with this question, "Those are big shoes to fill don't you think?"; my response was, "I am not going to try to fill their shoes. I am going to try to wear the ones the Lord gave me the best I can."

That is why I write this book, for some pastor who is facing the task of following a legendary leader. The Lord has called you to that place for such a time as this. Let the Lord develop you into the best you that you can be. This book will take a look into some elements of succeeding at succession in the local church. It is not exhaustive but can give insight into what may smooth what can be a rocky road. Your ministry is defined not by how you handle standing on shoulders of predecessors but how you handle leading and ministering in their shadows.

1

The Ideal

*I*t is difficult to follow a legendary leader. It has swallowed up the potential of many aspiring leaders throughout history. So imagine the enormous challenge facing Joshua. Joshua was following one of the most time-tested and skilled leaders of all time. Moses was extended a personal call from the Lord through a burning bush that was not consumed by its fire. Moses had a long and difficult history of leading a group of people who were not always thrilled by his leadership. Moses had faced mutinies and revolts and had endured the criticism and contention of those he led. And yet at the completion of his God-given task, he was respected and revered by the people. So much so that Deuteronomy 34:8 records that at his death, "the children of Israel wept for Moses in the planes of Moab thirty days." Thirty days was the customary period of mourning at the time of the text. Just because they mourned the customary thirty days, it does not mean that Moses's memory was swept away in thirty days.

It was with the memory of Moses fresh in the hearts and on the minds the children of Israel that Joshua takes the reins of leadership to guide the people into a Promised Land that was flowing with milk and honey. When looking at the succession model of Moses and Joshua, we see transition under near perfect circumstances. This is an example of what every church and organization would long for to secure its move into the future.

Training

There are immeasurable blessings and benefits to be able to learn to lead without all of the responsibilities and burdens of being the primary leader. These opportunities to be trained and prepared by a skilled leader are invaluable. Such is the case in this Moses-Joshua model.

Joshua was given the privilege of learning to lead in the real-life classroom of a legendary leader. God is so gracious to Joshua in this instance that all of the weight of leadership was not thrust upon him in one instantaneous moment. Joshua is given limited leadership responsibilities while watching Moses implement lifelong-learned leadership skills.

> And the Lord said to Moses: "Take Joshua the son of Nun with you, a man in whom is the Spirit, and lay your hand on him; set him before Eleazar the priest and before all the congregation, and inaugurate him in their sight. And you shall give some of your authority to him, that all the congregation of the children of Israel may be obedient. He shall stand before Eleazar the priest, who shall inquire before the Lord for him by the judgment of the Urim. At his word they shall go out, and at his word they shall come in, he and all the children of Israel with him—all the congregation (Num. 27:18–21, NKJV).

The training Joshua receives while observing Moses prepares him to lead and love the people. He is being trained by a monumental figure who brings him along as he teaches in both word and deed.

My undergraduate degree is in elementary education. The entire program and process while earning that degree required that I spend time in a classroom being taught how to teach because one day, I would be teaching. I learned curriculum, classroom management, lesson planning, and all of what was then cutting-edge educational theory. It was at the end of all of those classes about teaching that I would be given the opportunity to teach. This was afforded to me during a semester of what is called student teaching. This was not, however, the opportunity for the experienced permanent teacher to take a vacation. She slowly covered the course of a few weeks that allowed me to expand parts of the day for instruction. There came a time when for an entire week she turned the class over to me. Although I was no master teacher at that point, because of observation of and interaction with an experienced teacher, I was much better prepared. What had been learned in a college classroom, because of being trained by an experienced teacher, could now be put into practice in an elementary classroom.

It was similar with Joshua. He was prepared to lead because he had been trained by a legendary leader. Pastors and leaders trained by experienced pastors and experienced leaders will reap the harvest of the wisdom that has been sown while being trained.

Transference of Authority

Once again, the Moses-Joshua model is ideal. It is ideal because when transition occurs, there is more than likely the transference of authority. Much of the power and clout of the legendary leader is conveyed to the leader that has been trained because those who are being led identify the successor with the predecessor. As we will speak of later in the book, authority and influence are not given; they are gained. When the legendary leader believes in their successor enough to "lay their hands on them," there is a degree of authority that is transferred and attributed to the successor. This allows the leader to lead in a manner that would not otherwise be afforded them.

> Now Joshua the son of Nun was full of the spirit of wisdom, for Moses had laid his hands on him; so the children of Israel heeded him,

and did as the LORD had commanded Moses
(Deut. 34:9, NKJV).

The *New American Commentary* edited by Eugene H.
Merrill says this: "The formal act by which the community understood that Joshua was Moses' [*sic*] successor
was the ceremony of 'laying on of hands,'" a rite that
symbolized the transference of covenant authority and
responsibility from the one to the other. This physical
demonstration either accompanied the impartation of
the divine Spirit or marked the recipient as one already
endowed by that Spirit (verse nine). Thus, after Moses
had been told that he could not lead the people into
the Promised Land, he was told to "take Joshua son of
Nun, a man in whom is the spirit, and lay your hand on
him." The principal gift of the Spirit here was wisdom,
a necessary endowment if Joshua was to be able to take
Moses' place and successfully complete the conquest and
occupation of Canaan. The "spirit of wisdom" (i.e., the
spirit that bestows wisdom) appears elsewhere in the
scriptures. However, that ministry of the Spirit might
manifest itself in general, "*it was clear to Israel that Joshua*

was now properly certified and equipped to stand in Moses'
place as leader of the community."[1] (emphasis mine)

It was evident to Moses that God had chosen Joshua to be his successor. Moses had invested his time and leadership lessons in Joshua as well. Joshua had displayed loyalty and courage from what we can observe. And yet, as Moses prepares to transition from leading the children of Israel, it is necessary for him to lay hands on Joshua as a display of transferring his authority. Moses understood that, figuratively, simply giving Joshua the keys to the bus did not guarantee that Israel would get on board. Such is the case in many churches and organizations. Leadership appointment does not assure submission to leadership authority. The authority of the successor is strengthened when the outgoing leader endorses and sanctions the successor.

Transference of Vision

Vision for a church or organization is vital. To fail to cast vision is to prepare those you lead for failure and frustra-

---

1.   E. H. Merrill, *Deuteronomy*, Vol. 4 (Nashville: Broadman & Holman Publishers, 1994), 454–455.

tion. So much so that the Bible says, "Where there is no vision, the people perish" (Prov. 29:18, kjv).

The Bible also says that vision that is given by God must be plain so the one who reads it and proclaims it may run with it: "Then the Lord answered me and said: "Write the vision And make it plain on tablets, That he may run who reads it" (Hab. 2:2, nkjv).

A church or organization moves progressively forward when there is a vision that can be clearly communicated by its primary (principal) leader. That vision empowers those who are following the opportunity to focus on where the entire church is going. This benefits the whole church because it creates a consistency of planning, programming, and implementation. It creates a singularity of purpose.

Thus was the case as Moses passed the leadership mantle to Joshua. Although there may have at times been division among the people, there was never a question of the vision that was given to Israel's leaders. The single vision given to Israel's leaders was to inhabit the land that had been promised there foreparents in the faith.

> On this side of the Jordan in the land of Moab, Moses began to explain this law, saying, "The

LORD our God spoke to us in Horeb, saying: 'You have dwelt long enough at this mountain. Turn and take your journey, and go to the mountains of the Amorites, to all the neighboring places in the plain, in the mountains and in the lowland, in the South and on the seacoast, to the land of the Canaanites and to Lebanon, as far as the great river, the River Euphrates. See, I have set the land before you; go in and possess the land which the LORD swore to your fathers—to Abraham, Isaac, and Jacob—to give to them and their descendants after them'" (Deut. 1:1, 5–8; NKJV).

But the LORD was angry with me on your account, and would not listen to me. So the LORD said to me: "Enough of that! Speak no more to Me of this matter. Go up to the top of Pisgah, and lift your eyes toward the west, the north, the south, and the east; behold it with your eyes, for you shall not cross over this Jordan. But command Joshua, and encourage him and strengthen him; for he shall go over before this people, and he shall cause them to inherit the land which you will see." (Deut. 3:26–28, NKJV)

> Then Moses called Joshua and said to him in the sight of all Israel, "Be strong and of good courage, for you must go with this people to the land which the Lord has sworn to their fathers to give them, and you shall cause them to inherit it. And the Lord, He is the One who goes before you. He will be with you, He will not leave you nor forsake you; do not fear nor be dismayed" (Deut. 31:7–8, NKJV).

The vision was plain. Inhabit the land! The benefit for both the people and Joshua was that he had been taught by Moses who had received the vision. Additionally, because Joshua had inherited a God-given vision, there was no major change of course. The direction had been set, and Joshua was charged with completing what had started with Moses. And though their leadership styles and abilities may have differed, Joshua was the beneficiary of a divinely ordained destiny.

The ideal succession plan that Joshua experienced following a legendary leader like Moses was successful because of the hands-on training he received, the transference of authority observed by the people, and the transference of a stated and clear vision. These same elements can create an environment for effective pastoral succession. The succeeding pastor can, with confidence, lead the congregation because of these elements and flourish as the church moves smoothly forward.

2

The Realities the New Leader Faces

*I*n the prior chapter, I outlined the benefits of the succession model of Moses and Joshua. However, that model is not the experience of most who will follow legendary leaders in the local church or other organizations. Realistically, the vast majority of those who succeed legendary leaders will not have the benefit of sitting at the feet of a Moses–style leader who openly and willingly imparts wisdom, direction, and their authority. Most will be thrust into leadership without the advantage of contextual knowledge, a true measure of the emotional atmosphere, or the valuable unwritten, undocumented history of the institution. Candidates for leadership of churches and organizations are rarely given the keys to the closets where skeletons are buried. The antiseptic, sterile, and uncontaminated picture of a church or organization is the one that is painted for prospective leaders in anticipation of their arrival. Once they have occupied their office, the realities of the future relationship become clearer by the day.

These realities often expose challenges that are universal in their content but unique to their context. There are certain real challenges one will face when following legendary leaders that can be expected in any setting. The particulars of the environment are distinctive to each church or organization. Because the church is a spiritual entity is not an excuse to ignore the real human element that affects it. This human element provides both real opportunities and real challenges for the leader succeeding a legendary pastor.

The greatest reality an incoming pastor must accept and acknowledge is that just because you have been affirmed and given the title "pastor," it does not mean you are, in reality, the pastor. If you do a short etymology of pastor, you will find these origins: "shepherd, spiritual guide, shepherd of souls, herdsmen, to lead to pasture, set to grazing, cause to eat." It is the image of a shepherd who guides and leads sheep to a place they may graze and eat. Jesus, the Great Shepherd, makes a powerful statement in John 10: 27: "My sheep hear My voice, and I know them, and they follow Me" (John 10:27, NKJV).

The sheep know the voice of the shepherd, and they follow the shepherd. The reality is that when you are called as pastor, you have no sheep, except possibly your spouse and children. The new pastor has the privilege, responsibility, and extreme challenge of leading sheep who know the prior shepherd's voice—this will be covered later. In the excitement of the new charge, remember that reality.

This reality should not cause the new pastor to shirk their responsibility or escape the call. Remember, your predecessor, unless they founded the church, inherited their predecessor's sheep as well. This one reality kept clearly in mind will cause the new pastor to have an even greater internal celebration when the day arrives that they are pastor in title, in influence, and in authority.

I reiterate that most will not have the privilege of the Moses-Joshua succession model and therefore face realistic challenges in following legendary leaders. There are a few challenges I wish to highlight along with insights.

Lack of Influence

Initially, the new pastor must accept that the power and breadth of his influence is limited. This is not a matter of disrespect or contempt. It is, most of the time, a reality of unfamiliarity. Time and patience are the teammates of the new pastor.

Leadership expert John Maxwell says, "Leadership is Influence!" I would like to add that influence is gained (earned). Influence is not granted with the close of a church's pastoral search committee. Influence is gained within the close communion of the congregation. Influence is gained as the shepherd tends the sheep, even when they are not initially his.

Influence Is Gained by Commitment to the Lord's People

Greta Schacchi said, "A relationship requires a lot of work and commitment." Although she was not speaking of the relationship between a pastor and a congregation, the sentiment is applicable. The new pastor must convey their commitment to the congregation. This is not a blind promise to be with them until death. This commitment is a promise and pledge to lead and serve with intensity and integrity among them. The promise and pledge then must put on flesh and come alive through action and deed. Jean-Paul Sartre said, "Commitment is an act, not a word." The genuine desire to serve and lead can be discerned by a congregation. This allows influence to grow.

Influence Is Gained by Caring for the Lord's People

The old quote that is attributed to Theodore Roosevelt is still true: "People don't care how much you know until they know how much you care." Many a recent seminary graduate (present company included) marched into local churches with fresh textbooks full of principles on systematic theology, anthropology, soteriology, Christology, and all of the other -ologies you can think of. They entered with energy, excitement, and determination to save the world as they flooded sanctuaries with the latest philosophies and homiletic practices each Sunday morning. And while, the listening congregation may have been impressed by the knowledge being conveyed, they were not moved by the message being communicated. The pastor is to be the resident theologian; however, influence is gained by the pastor being present in the lives of the people. Care can be communicated from the pulpit to a limited extent. Care is most effectively displayed in hospital rooms and over coffee or in an emergency room. Care for a congregant is felt most powerfully when the crowd of Sunday morning is long gone and the pastor sits silently listening to the deep hurt of a parent grieving the loss of a wayward child. This kind of care cannot be measured in seconds or hours, but it can increase influence exponentially.

Influence Is Gained by Consistency with the Lord's People

Consistency for the new pastor is not a set schedule of office hours. Although to some, that may be a benefit. Consistency that gains influence is displayed through dependability and reliability. The new pastor will do great harm to their future if they try to be at every event, rehearsal, or meeting. It will set a standard that is almost impossible to maintain. However, to consistently be where you have said you will be when you said you will be there, positions you to have influence. Consistency is not just important with the new pastor's presence. It is even more important with your promises. As you are building relationships with those you lead, make as few promises as possible. Keep as many promises as you make. Your word is your bond. Those you lead will trust you when you have proven trustworthy. Lincoln Chafee said it this way: "Trust is built with consistency." Along with that, influence is gained by consistency of stewardship. The pastor's giving will lead giving. The congregation will ascertain how much you believe the vision by how you give toward the vision. Financial consistency and sacrifice must begin from the pulpit and from the new pastor's pocket. The new pastor cannot lead where they are not willing to go.

Influence Is Gained by Character among the Lord's People

The new pastor will have ample opportunities to exhibit and display character. And that won't always be in moments where the congregation has gathered. J. C. Watts says, "Character is doing the right thing when nobody's watching. There are too many people who think that the only thing that's right is to get by, and the only thing that's wrong is to get caught." The congregation will not always be privy to the moments when your character is being built, but they will be the judges of when results are revealed. The influence of the new pastor is strengthened when their integrity and honor are revealed in their deeds much more than their words. The congregation wants to know if you walk what you talk and that you live what you speak. This is built over time, through test, and in the midst of trials. Phillips Brooks, noted Episcopal rector of Boston's Trinity Church and lyricist of the Christmas hymn "O Little Town of Bethlehem," says, "Character may be manifested in the great moments, but it is made in the small ones."

Lack of Experience

John Keats says, "Nothing ever becomes real till it is experienced." Experienced preaching is not the same as experienced pastoring. Having a great itinerate ministry as an evangelist prepares you to some degree for the pulpit portion of being the new pastor. However, preaching does not take into account the multiple task of being the pastor. The experience of being the pastor only becomes real when it is personally experienced. Lack of experience is a reality that must be faced but does not have to be a liability or disadvantage. The exuberance and excitement that a lack of experience brings can energize a congregation in a unique way. Along with that, the naiveté and idealism of an inexperienced new pastor has catapulted many a church into staggering growth.

And yet, lack of experience is a reality that must be acknowledged by the new pastor, particularly the first-time pastor. Lack of experience is not dependent on the chronological age of the new pastor. Whether the new pastor is a youthful twenty something or a long-time ministerial associate in their first charge, lack of experience is a consideration. The examples of Timothy and Solomon regarding a lack of experience are very helpful to the new pastor.

The apostle Paul was aware of the place that lack of experience would play in the life of his protégé and mentee, Timothy. After being thrust into the position of primary pastoral leadership, Timothy would undoubtedly face the question of his lack of experience even though he had sat at the feet of the great apostle. Paul, therefore, leaves instructions for Timothy that can be summarized briefly: be an example and be prepared.

> Let no one despise your youth, but be an example to the believers in word, in conduct, in love, in spirit, in faith, in purity. Till I come, give attention to reading, to exhortation, to doctrine. Do not neglect the gift that is in you, which was given to you by prophecy with the laying on of the hands of the eldership. Meditate on these things; give yourself entirely to them, that your progress may be evident to all. Take heed to yourself and to the doctrine. Continue in them, for in doing this you will save both yourself and those who hear you (1 Tim. 4:12–16, NKJV).

Paul tells Timothy to not let anyone look down on his youthfulness. Paul then explains that this can be avoided by Timothy's example of Christian conduct. Paul seems to say to Timothy: "Your inexperience will be overshadowed by your life's conduct. Your inexperience will not be questioned when your character shows spiritual maturity." And likewise, Paul instructs Timothy to be prepared. "Give attention to reading, to exhortation, to doctrine." If you meditate and spend your time on these things, Paul says, your progress, growth, and maturity will be evident to all. The questions about inexperience can be, to some degree, nullified by the new pastor's life example and his preparation in the Word.

Solomon is another great model for those who lack experience in leading the Lord's people. Solomon in 1 Kings 3 is becoming the leader of a nation that has been led by a Hall of Fame of faithful leaders like Abraham, Moses, Joshua, Samuel, and David. Despite Solomon's lack of experience, he knows what to ask of the Lord that will enable him to lead as a godly leader.

> At Gibeon the Lord appeared to Solomon in a dream by night; and God said, "Ask! What shall I give you?"
>
> And Solomon said: "You have shown great mercy to Your servant David my father, because he walked before You in truth, in righteousness, and in uprightness of heart with You; You have continued this great kindness for him, and You have given him a son to sit on his throne, as it is this day. Now, O Lord my God, You have made Your servant king instead of my father David, but I am a little child; I do not know how to go out or come in. And Your servant is in the midst of Your people whom You have chosen, a great people, too numerous to be numbered

or counted. Therefore give to Your servant an understanding heart to judge Your people, that I may discern between good and evil. For who is able to judge this great people of Yours?"

The speech pleased the Lord, that Solomon had asked this thing. Then God said to him: "Because you have asked this thing, and have not asked long life for yourself, nor have asked riches for yourself, nor have asked the life of your enemies, but have asked for yourself understanding to discern justice, behold, I have done according to your words; see, I have given you a wise and understanding heart, so that there has not been anyone like you before you, nor shall any like you arise after you (1 Kgs. 2:5–12, NKJV).

Solomon acknowledges his lack of experience and asks the Lord for an understanding heart. "This phrase literally means 'a listening heart' or 'an obedient heart.' In the Old Testament 'hearing' and 'obeying' come from the same word, a linguistic trait with practical implications. Only those who obey authority figures have really *heard* them. Solomon must obey the Lord by keeping God's commands in order for his heart to be prepared to lead others. This listening to God will also enable him to listen to others."[2] For the new pastor, lack of experience is overcome by a willingness to first, listen to the Lord and the ability to listen to others.

Listening to the Lord may be easy for the new pastor. Listening to others may be more difficult. Learning from the experiences of others is a tool that often sits unused and underused in the toolbox of many new pastors. Douglass Adams—an English author, scriptwriter, satirist, and humorist—says, "Human beings, who are almost unique in having the ability to learn from the experiences of others, are also remarkable for their apparent disinclination to do so." The new pastor has vast libraries of lessons that can be learned if there is a willingness to listen to those who have survived what they are currently experiencing. Generally, the experienced pastor in your community that has served decades is not your enemy or "competition." The lessons of his service, both good and bad, can be vital information to the success of the new pastor. Reaching out to this experienced pastor will help the new pastor and honor the

---

2.   P. R. House, *1, 2 Kings*, Vol. 8 (Nashville: Broadman & Holman Publishers, 1995), 110.

experienced pastor. There are land mines in the church; I mean difficulties that can be avoided when an ear is opened and a heart is listening.

Lack of Exposure to a Successful Succession Model

Many new pastors face the reality of succeeding legendary leaders while lacking exposure that is beyond their control. Even if the new pastor has been in a congregational setting for years, some have not experienced firsthand a successful succession model. They have either served under a long-serving pastor, and therefore there was no need for a succession plan, or the successions they have witnessed have not been handled in a healthy manner.

As a result, the new pastor must prayerfully seek out a ministry mentor who has successfully navigated following a legendary leader. They are difficult but not impossible to find. John Crosby—who served as both in the United States House of Representatives and on the Massachusetts Supreme Judicial Court—says, "Mentoring is a brain to pick, an ear to listen, and a push in the right direction." Whether this is an invitation extended to lunch or an hour-long sit-down, it will be worth the time extending the invitation. Voltaire says, "Is there anyone so wise as to learn by the experience of others?"

3

The Reluctance of the Followers

*L*eading is relational. It is particularly so in the local church. As a result, the new pastor is at a disadvantage initially. This is because, generally, a new pastor has experienced a surface relationship with those he has been called to lead. Certainly, these relationships can be nurtured and deepened, but the reality is that it takes time. Because of this reality, there can be a reluctance of those in the congregation to follow the new leader. This reluctance can be overcome in time. But until then, the realities of this reluctance must be identified, systematically approached, and overcome.

Positional, Not Personal.

Many a new pastor has been destroyed by not identify-
ing this reality that is a part of a congregant or congregation's reluctance in following their leadership. When a
new pastor takes the congregation's reluctance as a personal assault, it creates damage that is difficult to repair.
It causes the pastor to avoid building relationships. It
creates distrust between the shepherd and the sheep.
This mind-set can prematurely weaken the relationship
between the pastor and lay leaders of the church. When
a pastor takes any question that is raised or any critique
that is voiced personally, it breaks the pastor's heart
because they are trying to lead in good faith and for the
good of the faithful.

The most damaging thing is that it can do irreparable
damage to the pastor's family. When a pastor feels as if
the reluctance of the congregation to follow their leadership is personal, they may believe the entire congregation is being critical. When this frustration and disappointment is communicated to the pastor's spouse and/
or family, it is a natural response to harbor ill will toward
the congregation. This unfortunate reality has severely
scarred scores of "first families" who have sacrificed to

serve and feel as if they have been betrayed by the very people they have been called to love and lead.

However, the truth is that on many occasions, the reluctance and hesitance that are displayed by congregations are not as a result of a personal dislike or distrust. The reluctance comes along with the position. Most times, the reluctance would occur no matter what person filled the position of pastor. The majority of caution a congregation has initially would be there if anyone other than Jesus was called to be their pastor. And it might take a few days for the Lord Himself!

Consider this. For the most part, a congregation only knows the new pastor by a résumé, an interview, word of mouth, and a few sermons as a candidate for the *position* of pastor. Admittedly, there are some wicked people who will take a personal dislike toward the new pastor just because of the sad state of their lives. However, most people in church display reluctance and resistance towards the *position* of the new pastor and not because of a personal dislike.

The new pastor must distinguish this early on or allow this misunderstanding to squeeze the small measure of joy and pleasure of leading the Lord's people. The new pastor must not allow the reluctance of those they lead to cause them to impulsively and hastily seek to move to the next station of ministry. They will quickly find that this same positional reluctance will greet them in the next pulpit, and they will have left behind the same for the Rev. Dr. John/Jane Doe that follows them.

A great example is once again the legendary leader and liberator, Moses. Most remembrances of Moses are of his heroic leadership, his pinpoint vision, and the exceptional love and dedication his followers had for him among other wonderful traits and qualities. We, however, do a disservice to his entire leadership career and character if we simply observe the successes. I believe even Moses faced the matter of reluctance from his followers that was positional and not personal. As he overcame this reluctance, his leadership was strengthened and the trust of his followers grew.

In Exodus 3, Moses has a burning bush experience where he encounters the presence of the Lord. The Lord calls Moses into service to lead the children of Israel from the oppressive bondage inflicted upon them by the Egyptian pharaoh. Reluctantly Moses accepts this leadership challenge. His first responsibility is to speak on behalf of the Lord to pharaoh about allowing the children of Israel to celebrate a pilgrim feast in the wilderness. Pharaoh responds by instructing the taskmasters to inform the children of Israel that they must continue the rate of production of bricks for construction but without the assistance of the Egyptians providing the straw that strengthened the bricks. Remember, Moses has met pharaoh with this message from the Lord at the behest of the Lord on behalf of the Lord's people. After pharaoh's announcement, we are given the opportunity to observe the response of the children of Israel.

> Then, as they came out from Pharaoh, they met Moses and Aaron who stood there to meet them. And they said to them, "Let the LORD look on you and judge, because you have made us abhorrent in the sight of Pharaoh and in the sight of his servants, to put a sword in their hand to kill us" (Exod. 5:20–21, NKJV).

This was not a personal attack on Moses. This was an attack on his position as the mouthpiece of the Lord. It did not matter that his name was Moses. What mattered was that he had upset the reasonably peaceable relationship between the children of Israel and pharaoh. His name could have been Aaron, Caleb, or Joshua. Whoever would have caused this uproar would have received the wrath of the children of Israel. Even in this biblical instance, their reluctance in seeing where Moses was leading them was positional and not personal.

I remember vividly within a month of beginning my pastorate of the Shiloh Baptist Church of Dayton, Ohio, receiving a request for an appointment from one of the long-standing and well-respected members. She and her husband had been faithful members for decades. The meeting was one that I cherish in hindsight. This godly woman entered my office and began a monologue that evolved into a dialogue.

"Reverend Bachus, I have been a member of this church as long as you have been alive. And I was here when you got here, and I will be here when you are gone. Now, I want you to know that I did not vote for you, and I am not happy that you are here. And I am going to continue to teach my class and support my church. But I wanted you to know that I voted for the other candidate, and I still want him to be my pastor even though you are here."

Initially, her statement caught me off guard. I was not prepared for what she had just said. It was only the grace of God and the direction of His Holy Spirit that guided my response.

"Thank you for requesting this time with me. I want to first, say thank you for saying this directly to me and not sowing seeds of discord with others in the congregation. I also want to say that you don't know me, and I don't know you. So any ill will you have toward me is unfounded. I am not surprised that you did not vote for me because you don't know me. And the pastor you voted for is a great preacher and a kind man. Again, I want to thank you for coming directly to me. And one more thing before you go, in three or four years, there will be people who are rejoicing that I am here today, will wish they never saw me. And others who wished I had never arrived will be my biggest supporters and most faithful followers."

The relationship I have with that same godly lady has grown to be full of love. Even after being gone for a decade, each time I see her in Dayton, Ohio, she greets me with a kiss, a hug, and loving words. I knew that day that her reluctance about me being the pastor was not a personal issue she had with me. It was positional. Whomever the church would have called would have received the same conversation if it were not her preferred preacher.

The new pastor must recognize that some initial reluctance from the congregation is not personal. It is directed at the person that inherits the position. Once again, time and patience are the best teammates of the new pastor. As you show the congregation the commitment and integrity of the *person* that possesses the *position*, reluctance has the tendency to be reduced.

Loyalty to Prior Pastors

"My sheep hear My voice, and I know them, and they follow Me" (John 10:27, NKJV).

This is a powerful and profound statement that Jesus makes in John 10. Clearly, Jesus is speaking in John 10 in the context of teaching of His relationship with His followers and in the context of being challenged about His claim as Christ. And yet John 10 has some teachable tenets and principles that are applicable to the new pastor.

The first of which is the new pastor is the privileged beneficiary of inheriting the sheep of a previous shepherd. If the church is not one founded by the new pastor, the new pastor is given the honor and challenge of learning to lead another shepherd's sheep. And whether that shepherd is in the building, in another church, or in glory, those sheep continue to know that shepherd's voice. And will, to some degree, continue to follow.

The second powerful principle is found in earlier verses of John 10.

> But he who enters by the door is the shepherd of the sheep. To him the doorkeeper opens, and the sheep hear his voice; and he calls his own sheep by name and leads them out. And when he brings out his own sheep, he goes before them; and the sheep follow him, for they know his voice. Yet they will by no means follow a stranger, but will flee from him, for they do not know the voice of strangers (John 10:2–5, NKJV).

What a shocking revelation and reality. For many in the congregation, the new pastor has the voice of a stranger while the past pastor has the voice of the shepherd.

This is not a reason to resign, and yet it is a reason to take a reality check. There is an inherent and natural loyalty individual congregants and the collective congregation have for a departed pastor. It is instantly recognized in the imagery of John 10 verses two through five. The sheep hear the shepherd's voice. The shepherd calls the sheep by name. The shepherd brings out his own sheep. The sheep follow the shepherd because they know his voice.

This is the image of a shepherd that leads, cares for, and interacts with the sheep. It is that relationship that cultivates and develops a loyalty to the pastor. When a congregation has heard the voice of the shepherd preaching, teaching, and counseling during both good and bad times, loyalty grows. The shepherd's presence when babies are dedicated and when loved ones are laid to rest creates a deep loyalty. When the shepherd speaks in prayer in the courtroom, and hospital room, it generates allegiances that are not easily forged or forgotten.

There is something to say about the past pastor and their ability to aid the new pastor. A secure past pastor does not need the continued affirmation of his former congregants to fill some empty space in their ego. You can observe the maturity of a true shepherd because they do not become meddlesome agents of discord and division in the churches they have served. They know this has the possibility to destroy the foundation and work they have built through their efforts and the Lord's blessings. A past shepherd of integrity will minimize his voice being heard in order to not hinder the new pastor's leadership.

The new pastor would be wise to recognize these loyalties as realities that will likely be encountered. Fighting these loyalties openly is not wise. It displays some measure of insecurity and uncertainty about your call. Don't be defeated by the ghost of pastors' past. Accept the reality of this loyalty and do not allow the enemy to convince you that desecrating and denigrating your predecessor's legacy is a proper approach to this loyalty.

This kind of loyalty is, in all reality, not a slap in the face of the new pastor. It should actually be a motivator for serving the congregation. The congregation's loyalty to the past pastor is an indication that this is a congregation that has the desire to follow and the ability to love leadership. Consider the congregation's loyalty to the past pastor as a preview of their future love for the new pastor. With time and patience, you can become as revered as your predecessor.

Loyalty to Long-standing Relationships

This is a far more dangerous animal. The new pastor is given the opportunity to build relationships over time in the congregation. The reality is that while these relationships are being built, others are simply aging. As the newcomer, the new pastor is only aware of obvious relationships among the congregation: husbands and wives, parents and children, ministry leader and ministry participants, and so on. Add to these obvious relationships many relationships that are unknown to the new pastor and may only be revealed over time. Long-lasting relationships within the congregation produce deep loyalty as well. These relationships are not necessarily bad, but they can, at times, become a hindrance to the leadership of the new pastor.

The new pastor must navigate being placed in this context carefully. The instruction of Jesus to His disciples as He sends them into new ministry settings in Matthew 10 will serve the new pastor well. "Behold, I send you out as sheep in the midst of wolves. Therefore be wise as serpents and harmless as doves" (Matt. 10:16, NKJV).

I don't want to give the impression that congregants are wolves. However, there are those that have wolf-like tendencies at times. The wisdom necessary to navigate long-lasting relationships should be on the prayer list of every new pastor.

I raise the reality of this loyalty to long-standing relationships because the mutual respect many congregants have for one another or leaders within the congregation, if not used for good and godly reasons, can hinder the leadership of the new pastor. We can never dismiss the human factor in the spiritual setting of the churches in which we operate. Pride, haughtiness, and conceit has the ability to subtly and slyly sneak into the hearts and minds of the best member of a congregation when they feel they are right and the new pastor is wrong. It is under these conditions that these alliances of long-lasting relationships are called upon to influence the direction of the church away from the new pastor's vision.

The new pastor does themselves a disservice if they do not acknowledge the reality of these long-standing relationships. Although they may not be identifiable as the new pastor begins to serve, they will begin to surface as time passes. As the new pastor observes the participation of congregants in "meetings before the meeting" and "meetings after the meeting" these relationships will begin to be identified. Also, when the new pastor receives comments and commentary from a congregant from a consultation, appointment, or meeting the congregant was not involved in personally, these connections begin to reveal themselves. The loyalty nurtured by these long-standing relationships should not automatically alarm the new pastor in a negative way. It is just wise to understand that years of loyalty among members of the congregation, in most times, trump their relationship with the new pastor.

The new pastor must take into account these long-standing relationships and how they influence the growth of the congregation. These relationships are not always characterized by love and harmony. Adversaries can align long enough to defeat what is perceived as a common enemy or threat. Remember the Pharisees and Sadducees were diametrically opposed in their theological and philosophical thoughts and practices. And yet, when Jesus threatened their authority and influence, he became a common target they both aimed for.

Be careful of trusting or testing relationships until you have an idea of preexisting relationships. There are unknowns that go unspoken until loyalties are tested and tried. It is like a tea bag—the true contents of relationships are, many times, only revealed in the heat of conflict, crisis, and contention. True loyalties are rarely revealed in seasons of calm and peace. The Lord will reveal these long-standing relationships and the roadblocks they have the potential to create. It is the new pastor's responsibility to pray for discernment to identify them and the sensitivity to manage ministry around them.

4

Moving Forward in Faith

*T*he new pastor benefits from standing on the shoulders of the preceding legendary pastor. The facilities inherited, the gathered congregation, and the history that has been made are a result of the leadership, sacrifice, and vision of the preceding pastor. All that has been built physically and intangibly are a result of the favor the Lord displayed in the life of that prior pastor and the following congregation. It is the privilege of the new pastor to stand proudly on what has been built.

However, there are looming shadows that will be present as well. It is in the darkness and sometimes cold of these shadows that the new pastor must live, minister, and lead. And unless the preceding pastor organized the church, they have had the experience of spending time in the shadow of a legendary leader. This is evidence that shadows can successfully be navigated.

A word to the wise: never fully fall prey to the enemy's ploy of playing the comparison game. The congregation, community, and other clergy will spend plenty of time playing this game themselves. The new pastor will hear it in conversations, experience it in comments, and even see it in social media. This is a game the new pastor can never win. In their absence, the preceding pastor is deified or vilified. Do not fall into the harmful habit of comparing yourself to a person who is not present. The new pastor will either have a self-esteem problem or a pride problem. If the preceding pastor was gifted in all manner of pastoral responsibilities, your shortcomings in one area will convict, haunt, and humiliate the new pastor. If the preceding pastor was a complete failure, your successes will cause the new pastor to think highly of themselves. Allow those who will play this hurtful and divisive game, and simply be assured that the preceding pastor was present for "such a time as this" and so are you.

The new pastor must approach their charge and challenges spiritually, strategically, and confidently. These are the approaches that will allow the new pastor to move forward even when occupying the shadow of a predecessor.

Spiritually

Pray! Prayerfully, every new pastor will develop a deep and consistent prayer life. Leading the Lord's people will force you to have a consistent prayer life; or burnout, disappointment, and dysfunction will follow. The challenges, personalities, egos, tragedies, and triumphs of those served by the new pastor will necessitate conversations with the Lord. The questions, frustrations, and disappointing experiences of the new pastor should not drive them crazy. It should drive them to their knees. However, there are three specific prayers I suggest the new pastor lift on at least a weekly basis to the Lord.

First, the new pastor needs to pray that the Lord develops within them a pastor's heart. The following prayer requests are a part of this, but I want to separate and delineate them. When we think of a pastor's heart, we normally think of a heart for ministry, a heart for people, and a heart for the Lord. All of these are a part of the makeup of a pastor's heart. A pastor's heart includes, as well, the ability and willingness to be among the Lord's people, a shepherd among his sheep. I am not suggesting a careless familiarity with the congregation. I am suggesting, as best as possible, to know the hurts, hang-ups, joys, sorrows, and victories of those the new pastor leads. Pray for the ability to nurture the kinds of relationships that a congregant can enter your office and share the deepest, darkest secrets of their lives, and they are confident in your confidentiality enough that they know when you see them in the life of the congregation, you will approach them just as you would the person on the pew next to them and not reveal their weaknesses and struggles. The new pastor will not quickly know the names of each congregant. The new pastor can, however, inquire about their family, jobs, and pursuits. This kind of interest engenders trust and loyalty. Pray for a pastor's heart.

Second, pray the Lord provides the ability to love unconditionally. As a realist, I know that this is almost impossible to do absolutely. It can be something that is practiced as much as possible. The new pastor should pray that the love he displays is not simply to those who are influential and outstanding. Pastoral love and care is desired and needed most by those who silently struggle to live through the challenges that face them even if they are not upfront. Additionally, the new pastor should seek to display pastoral love to those who are supportive as well as those who question his leadership. It is surprising but true that many who are derisive and divisive in congregations are that way because of what they are lacking in their own lives. The new pastor has the possibility of transforming a perceived enemy into an ally if they show love and care in spite of the person's actions and personality. Pray for the ability to love unconditionally.

Third, pray for the Lord to enable you to forgive when you have been wronged. The new pastor will be wronged whether intentionally or unintentionally. How the wrong is handled will send strong signals to the congregation about the spiritual makeup of their new leader. Prayer before reacting to being wronged is always the proper order. If the new pastor does not seek to forgive when wronged, they will face many instances when they are required to minister to those who have wronged them. Imagine carrying the hurt and disappointment of being wronged when you have to marry a person's daughter who has wronged you, or you are visiting a sick person who has negatively spoken about you, or even as you are counseling a spouse whose other half has questioned your motives for ministry. When hurts go unforgiven, it hinders the new pastor's ability to fully and faithfully represent the One who called and assigned them. Father Lawrence G. Lovasik—teacher, author, and founder of Sisters of the Divine Spirit—says, "Strength of character means the ability to overcome resentment against others, to hide hurt feelings, and to forgive quickly."

Pray for a pastor's heart. Pray the Lord provides the ability to love unconditionally. Pray the Lord enables you to forgive when you have been wronged.

Strategically

Pray! The subject of this prayer is for a discerning spirit and insightful wisdom. The new pastor must clearly understand that leadership and growth cannot be accomplished by ability and energy. It requires co-laborers and coleaders. The new pastor must accept the responsibility of most of the labor and most of the leadership, but great things for the Kingdom cannot be accomplished through one person.

The new pastor should pray that the Lord identifies and places a burden in the life of "bridge leaders." Bridge leaders are congregants who, because of their influence and respect, are able to bridge the time between the new pastor's arrival and the time the pastor gains the trust, respect, and confidence of the congregation. These leaders may be official leaders who hold positions and titles, or they may be well-respected congregants who have no official position.

The new pastor should pray that the Lord reveals these bridge leaders who can play a huge part assisting the new pastor to become *the* pastor. These leaders are people with godly character and integrity. And most importantly, they must have a love for the Lord and His church more than they love being loved. Their stand with the new pastor will sometimes make them unpopular and shunned.

A bridge leader will stand for what is right when others will declare, "We have never done it that way before." A bridge leader respects the fact the congregation prayed that the Lord would send a pastor after His own heart.

That leader, as well, believes that if the Lord has placed the new pastor, they deserve prayer, support, and assistance. A bridge leader sees the bigger picture and the future. This kind of leader is not in it for personal gain or glory but for the glory of God and Kingdom building.

Jethro, the father-in-law of Moses, was a bridge leader. He observed Moses in an overwhelming circumstance trying to teach and guide a vast multitude that had been released from Egyptian bondage. Jethro, because of his wisdom and experience, knew that this was a fruitless effort and would drain Moses of his leadership energy. Jethro, a bridge leader himself, suggested that Moses identify other bridge leaders that would assist him with the tasks at hand.

> Moreover you shall select from all the people able men, such as fear God, men of truth, hating covetousness; and place such over them to be rulers of thousands, rulers of hundreds, rulers of fifties, and rulers of tens (Exod. 18:21, NKJV).

Jethro was willing to assist the primary leader because he saw the need and how his assistance would further the work of the Lord. Nowhere is it recorded that Jethro asked for favors or something in return. Jethro did not hold the wisdom he had provided over the head of Moses. He simply saw a leader of the Lord's people who needed a bridge to effectively cross to effective leadership. These are the kinds of leaders the new pastor should pray for.

Confidently

Pray! The new pastor must pray for confidence in the call and assignment they have responded to—confidence that the Lord has led them to this place of service. Confidence should not be confused with arrogance. Samuel Butler, Victorian-era author, says, "The truest characters of ignorance are vanity and pride and arrogance." The confidence the new pastor has can be based on the thought that this is not arrogance. I am confident in my assignment. After prayerful considerations by both candidate and congregation have affirmed on earth what the Lord has confirmed in heaven should allow the new pastor to be sure of their new assignment. This does not assume that there will not be difficulties. It should hearten, encourage, and strengthen the resolve of the new pastor if there is a confidence that this assignment has been endorsed by the Lord.

Once again, the relationship between two biblical legendary leaders is a great example of the reason the new pastor can have confidence in their new assignment. As was mentioned earlier, Joshua had the benefit of being mentored by one of the unquestioned greatest leaders in history. Joshua had the privilege of observing the leadership excellence of Moses (and some of Moses's mistakes as well). It was after this lengthy role as mentee that Joshua was handed the reins of leadership to bring to a conclusion the exodus from Egypt and the conquering of the Promised Land. It is at this point that the Lord speaks to Joshua words that every new pastor should depend on in their new assignment when following a legendary leader.

> After the death of Moses the servant of the LORD, it came to pass that the LORD spoke to Joshua the son of Nun, Moses' [*sic*] assistant, saying: "Moses My servant is dead. Now therefore, arise, go over this Jordan, you and all this people, to the land which I am giving to them— the children of Israel. Every place that the sole

of your foot will tread upon I have given you, as I said to Moses. From the wilderness and this Lebanon as far as the great river, the River Euphrates, all the land of the Hittites, and to the Great Sea toward the going down of the sun, shall be your territory. No man shall be able to stand before you all the days of your life; *as I was with Moses, so I will be with you. I will not leave you nor forsake you* (Josh. 1:1–5, NKJV; emphasis mine).

Imagine the confidence and comfort Joshua experienced after hearing these words from the Lord! "As I was with Moses, so I will be with you. I will not leave you nor forsake you." These are the words that gave Joshua the confidence to lead the children of Israel into what had been promised to their forefathers centuries before. What the Lord was conveying to Joshua is that ultimately, this was His work and His plan. That gave Joshua the confidence and courage to lead Israel. It was not the training at the feet of Moses. It was the assurance of the presence of the Lord as he gave leadership.

The new pastor must have that kind of confidence in their assignment—the confidence that the Lord is with them and this assignment is a part of the plan of the Lord. Notice, the Lord was not denying the leadership successes of Moses. He was simply affirming His abiding presence with Joshua. The new pastor must be confident that just as the Lord was with the prior pastor, the Lord is with them as well.

I am reminded of my call to the Salem Baptist Church of Omaha, Nebraska. Salem was then and has been for the last sixty-five years the largest African-American congregation in the State of Nebraska. It is internationally known for the powerful preaching that occupies its pulpit and the masterful music of its Music Ministry. I had been familiar with Salem as a youth because Dr. J. C. Wade Sr., the pastor at the time, would often have my father and the church he led to come to worship with Salem. The legacy of this great leader was yet alive. I was also familiar with the international preaching acclaim of the pastor I would succeed, Pastor Maurice Watson. I not only knew him from afar, but he had preached revival for me at the Shiloh Baptist Church of Dayton, Ohio, on two occasions. To say that following these legends was intimidating would be an understatement.

Then came the first Sunday of my pastoral career at Salem. After a much-anticipated first Sunday, I exited the sanctuary escorted by two deacons who stood by my side as I greeted those who attended worship. At that point, a reporter from the city's newspaper approached me and began to recall the great leaders I was blessed to follow. She then capped it off with this statement, "You have some really big shoes to fill."

I paused and remembered my father saying to me, "Selwyn, no one can be you better than you." And in response to the reporter I said, "Yes, those are big shoes. However, I am not going to try to fill their shoes, I am going to try to wear the shoes the Lord gave me the best I can."

For more information contact:

Pastor Selwyn Q. Bachus
C/O Advantage Books
P.O. Box 160847
Altamonte Springs, FL 32716

info@advbooks.com

To purchase additional copies of this book visit our bookstore website at: ww.advbookstore.com

Longwood, Florida, USA
"we bring dreams to life"™
www.advbookstore.com